TECHNICAL MANUAL

for

Rifle, U.S. Type 99 Japanese Cal. .30

三 八 式 歩 兵 銃

全 體

Technical Manual for Rifle U.S. Type 99 Japanese Cal. .30

ISBN - 978-0934523684

Editor@Middle-Coast-Publishing.com

Middle-Coast-Publishing.com

Reprinting of this Training Manual is dedicated to the inventor of the legendary Arisaka Rifle, Lieutenant Colonel Arisaka Nariakira of the Imperial Japanese Army.

Preface

During the Korean War, approximately 126,500 short and 6,650 long Japanese Type 99 Arisaka Rifles were re-chambered under American supervision at the Tokyo arsenal to fire the U.S. Military M2 -.30-06 Springfield cartridge.

These rifles were fitted with a lengthened magazine well and had a small notch cut in the top of the receiver ring in order to accommodate the .30-06 round's 1/3 of an inch greater overall length.

The Pentagon rather wisely wrote a Technical Manual for the converted rifles that addresses inspection of the weapon, care, assembly and function. This then is that 1950s era TM.

Rather than merely photocopy it and be done with it, our editors took the time and trouble to retype the manuscript from cover to cover. As a result, instead of a washed out, hard to read text, it is crystal clear. We also corrected some of the original typos and cleaned up the grammar to it is easier to read and easier to understand what the DoD author is trying to say.

The Editors

CONTENTS

TECHNICAL MANUAL

For

Rifle, U.S. Type 99, Japanese Cal. .30

Chapter 1. Rifle
I Construction

A. Barrel Group

1. The inside of the barrel is divided into a rifled section, chamber and a bolt face seat. The rifled section consists of four right twist rifling's whose land surface is chrome plated. The chamber is shaped to fit the cartridge and its rear portion is rounded to form a bolt face seat.

The bolt face seat aids in guiding the ammunition and has an extractor groove on the right side. The outside surface of the rear end of bolt face seat is threaded. After the receiver is screwed on to the barrel, it is aligned with the marker.

2. The rear sight base is mounted on the rear of the barrel and is prevent from moving by a small sight base screw and a small rear sight spring screw.

The rear sight leaf is pivoted by a rear sight joint pin and maintains lowered and raised positions through rear sight spring action. The rear sight leaf is graduated from 300 to 1500 meters by etched lines spaced into 100 meter units. Both sides of the rear sight leaf are notched at the above- mentioned intervals to engage the rear sight slide catch when the upper of the slide coincides with the previously mentioned etched lines. The circular peep sight formed, at the bottom by lowering the rear eight leaves is used for firing at ranges of 100 meters, The semi-circular peep sight is formed by raising the rear right leaf and slide is used for firing ranges of 200 meters.

The forward edge of the rear sight leaf spring is dovetailed and fits into the rear sight base. It is held in place by set screws. The projection on the upper surface prevents the rear right leaf from moving to the right or left. The spring is curved upward so that it constantly averts upward pressure on the lower end of the rear right leaf.

The slide is inserted onto the rear sight leaf and is held the desired position by means of a spring loaded catch. The rear sight set screws on the upper right side prevents the slide from slipping off. The spring loaded slide catch is screwed on each side of the slide by slide pin. The center peep sight is aligned with the front sight for firing ranges of 300 to 1500 meters.

The catch of the slide through the action of the spring engages the grooves or both sides of the rear sight leaf and holds the slide in its various elevated positions. On each side and at the back of the slide is an antiaircraft leaf sight arm. The antiaircraft lead sight arm has two scaled notches: 2 and 3, at the bottom. Notch 2 is used for firing on aircraft traveling direct horizontal distances for 600 yards at speeds of 125 miles per hour and notch 3, at speeds of 185 miles per hour. The anti-aircraft lead sight arm is attached by antiaircraft lead arm screws. The spring attached to the bottom holds the antiaircraft arm in folded and extended positions. During its operation the aircraft is aligned with front and rear sight and fired upon when it enters the proper notch on the bottom of the anti-aircraft lead sight arm.

4. The front sight blade is dovetailed tightly into the front sight base. The front sight base pin which is inserted from left to right. The line formed with the front sight base and the front sight is determined by zeroing. Two shoulders which project upward from the front sight base serve as guards for the sight blade.

B. Receiver Group

6. The receiver houses the bolt. The upper surface of the receiver has two gouged holes. The one which cut out from the top to the right side serves as a receive port during loading and as an ejection port after firing. The cartridge clip housing is formed by the rear section. The other hole serves as a path for the bolt handle. It is slanted towards the front end to facilitate the action of the bolt when it is pulled back.

There is a long narrow recess along each side of the receiver in which the bolt rides. Serial number of the rifle and the name of the manufacture are engraved below the groove on the left side. A slot which engages the bolt retainer base and lip of ball retainer, and an ejector groove are found on the rear left side.

The sear pin is located to the rear of the rectangular opening at the bottom. The safety lock hole is located on the forward section of the sear pin seat and firing pin catch hole in the rear section. The forward and rear receiver lugs are drilled for long and short receiver screws. The screws are used to attach the trigger guard to the receiver. The buffer and recoil plate are attached to forward and rear lugs, respectively, and serve to transmit recoil shock to the stock during firing.

On each side of the inner surface is a longitudinal groove which permits the riding of bolt locking lug and extractor. The forward portion of the groove is widened to house the bolt locking lug. On the op surface of this housing is a gas port which permits gas to escape. An engraved crest is located in the forward portion of the gas port, and an engraved figure TYPE 99, reading from left to right, is located to the rear of the gas port.

The front end of the inside groove is also widened to provide passage for the bolt retaining lug. At the rear of the receiver there is a groove for the lug on the safety knob and another groove for the sear catch. A groove on which the safety catch lug rides is located in the extended portion of the receiver. This groove curves to the left and serves as a guide and lock for the safety catch lug when the rifle is set in safety position.

6. Receiver attachments consist of bolt latch, ejector, sear, trigger and recoil plate.

7. The Bolt retaining latch assembly fits on the left side of the receiver. The sear catch always projects out through the action of bolt retaining latch spring attached to the bolt retainer. It engages the bolt retaining luge and limits the backward movement of the bolt. In order to remove the bolt from the receiver, the bolt retaining latch is pulled out to disengage the catch. The ejector is attached to the bolt retaining latch assembly by the latch screw and projects into the ejector groove of the receiver by the action of ejector spring attached to the bolt retaining latch spring.

When the bolt is brought to the rear, the ejector riding on the ejector groove strikes the bottom of the cartridge and throws the cartridge out to the right. The catch of the bolt retaining latch gives proper position to the ejector when the bolt is removed.

8. The sear has a firing pin catch on the rear end sand a safety lock on the front end and is attached to the sear pin seat of the receiver by means of the sear pin.

The trigger is attached to the sear with a trigger pin and forms a large and small wavelike knoll. The large knoll engages the lower surface of the receiver and adjust the projection of the firing pin catch within the receiver. The catch on the front end engages the bottom of the sear and sets the position of the trigger. The sear spring encircling the safely lock pivots around the sear pin and always holds the firing pin catch in projected position within the receiver.

When the trigger is pulled to the first phase (when trigger play is taken up0 the sear spring is forced, and the big knoll turns while engaging the lower surface of the receiver. Simultaneously with the engage of the knoll with the l woe surface of the receiver, the firing pin catch is lowered to a certain extent. When the trigger is pulled to the second phase (when the sear is engaged), the sear spring is subjected to further pressure, the firing pin catch is lowered further and the safety lock is placed in the safety groove of the receiver. Through such action of the safety lock, safety section is created. In short, the opening of the bolt handle is prevented during discharge and the pulling of the trigger is prevented when the rifle is half-cocked.

9. The recoil plate is attached to the rear of the receiver. The rear lug the receiver is inserted into the forward hold. It is connected to the trigger guard by screwing the trigger guard screw into the threaded hole in the rear end. Together with the buffer, it transmits recoil to the stock during discharge. Furthermore, together with the trigger guard it strengthens the rifle grip.

C. Bolt

10. The bolt consisting of the following parts is attached to the receiver: Bolt housing, firing pin, firing pin spring, safety catch, extractor and bolt cover.

11. The bolt housing contains a firing pin chamber forward portion of which is recessed to limit the forward motion of the firing pin during firing.

The front end of its head is called the breech surface. The embanked lug at the head functions together with the extractor until the cartridge is extracted. The lugs on both sides of the head are called the bolt locking catches and the lug to the rear of the left bolt locking lug is called the bolt retaining lug. The narrow groove extending through the center of the groove connects with the firing pin chamber and permits gas to escape from the primer. The bolt retaining lug engages the bolt retainer and limits the backward movement of the bolt. The elliptical hole midway between the bolt locking lugs and toward its rear permits the gas to escape from the bolt housing and at the same time indicates position for assembling the extractor.

The extractor collar which adjoins the bolt retaining lug is attached to the extractor and permits natural turning. Two shallow grooves on to the right front and one to the bottom front of the bolt handle, are found on the bolt housing. The right front groove is in the slot for the safety locking during firing and the bottom front is for the safety lug during the backward movement of the bolt when the rear catch presses the ear down. Approximately one –half of the circumference to the seat is cut off in fork shape. The elongated cut-off is called the snail-shaped section the shorter cut-off is called the semi-circular section. The snail-shaped section, together with the turning of the bolt housing serves to withdraw the firing pin as it engages the sear catch and its bottom portion becomes the slot for the sea catch during firing. The semicircular section becomes the slot for the sear catch when the firing pin is withdrawn. A collar on the rear end of the bolt housing engages the groove on the insides of the safety knob and holds the bolt hosing and the safety knob together.

A small projection at the rear of the bolt handle engages the notch cut into the outside of the safety know, and ruing safety, together with the safety catch prevents the bolt from opening.

The firing pin assembly, consisting of striker and the firing pin spring operates in the firing pin chamber of the bolt housing. The right, inside surface at the rear of the firing pin has a longitudinal groove terminating at the square opening in its forward end. This opening is connected to the long narrow opening on the upper surface. These grooves and openings serve as passages from the projection on the safety knob shaft during assembly and disassembly. Furthermore, the long narrow opening serves as a passage for the projection on the safety knob shaft during the forward motion of the firing pin and prevents the firing pin from turning freely. The projecting portion at the rear of the ring pin is called the sear catch. The sear catch engages the firing pin catch and compresses the firing pin spring. The small circular port in front is a gas escape.

13. The firing pin spring housed in the firing pin spring chamber activates the firing pin and maintains the position of the safety device.

14. The safety knob connects with the bolt housing and the firing pin and engages the safety device. The rear portion of the knob is knurled with a small semicircular notch at the left side and safety knob lug at the bottom. The safety knob lug fits into the groove at the end of the receiver and prevents the safety knob from turning.

When the safety knob is locked by pressing the safety knob forward and turning the safety knob lug to the left during cocked position of the bolt, the right side of the notched section on the outside of the safety k now engages the small projection on the rear of the bolt handle and prevents the raising of the bolt handle. One half of the inner circumferences has a shelf-like recess which engages the collar on the rear of the bolt housing and causes it to function together with the firing pin spring.

The safety knob shaft is the principal element in the bolt assembly. The projection on the center of the shaft fits into the long, narrow groove and opening of the firing pin spring chamber and facilitates the assembly of the bolt. During assembly, together with the safety knob lug, it prevents the firing pin from turning.

The safety device turns the firing pin to the right, engages the sear catch to the left sear slot of the receive rand prevents connection between the sear and the firing pin.

15. The extractor is a flat piece under spring tensions. Its tip engages the rear end of the cartridge and extracts it. The projected section to the rear of the tip fits into the groove at the head of the bolt casing which prevents it from slipping forward.

The hollowed portion on the back surface of the extractor engages the projected portion of the extractor collar and holds the extractor to the bolt housing. When the bolt handle is opened, the extractor remains in the right, inside groove of the receiver without being affected by the turning of the bolt housing since the extractor collar turns freely.

16. Since the bolt cover is attached to the receiver by means of bent tips on both sides, it

covers the upper surface of the receiver and prevents dust from entering the receiver.

D. Magazine

17. The magazine consists of magazine body, trigger guard and their accessories. The body is box shaped and contains a follow and a magazine spring. It is used for loading ammunition. The front and back of the magazine are attached to the trigger guard to prevent it from slipping out of the stock.

18. The trigger guard forms a seat for the magazine and serves as a shield for the trigger and as a re-enforcement for the stock grip. It is attached to the bottom of the stock with three small screws. The long mouth towards the front holds the bottom end of the magazine. The floor plate catch housing is located at the rear section of the long mouth.

The short screw hole for the receiver is located the forward tip of the trigger guard. The trigger guard screw and a rectangular hole are found at the rear end and center respectively. Thus, room for operation of trigger is provided. The semicircular guard which protects the trigger has a small hole in the front and ad as a recess for the floor plate catch. A long setscrew hole in the front end as a recess for the floor plate catch. A long setscrew hold for the receiver is located at the other end.

19. The trigger guard accessories consists of the follower, magazine spring, floor plate, floor plate catch, trigger guard screws and the long and short set screws for the receiver.

20. The follower is a long, narrow, plate, the top surface which is angled. It is contained in the magazine and together with the magazine spring, raises the ammunition in the magazine upward. A clamp for holding the magazine spring is located in the front underside of the follower.

21. The magazine spring is an E-shaped flat spring, the narrow end of which is attached to the follow. The other end is connected to the floor plate. It constantly exerts s pressure to raise the ammunition in the magazine.

22. The front end of the floor plate is attached to the front end of the trigger guard magazine opening by means of a small pin. A small recess in the center of the floor plate engages the floor plate catch and prevents it from opening. A lip is provided at the back of the floor plate for inserting one end of the magazine spring.

23. The floor plate catch is attached to the floor palate catch housing the trigger guard. It consists of a body, screw and a spring. It is]-shaped and operated in the groove located in the forward end of the trigger guard semicircular section and is attached to the trigger guard by a small screw.

The bottom front section of the catch has a claw and the rear section is inletted. A small hole in the center of the body is used as a catch hook for a tool when the floor plate catch cannot be released by finger. An elliptical hole on the top surface of the body, together with a small screw, controls the movement of the floor plate catch.

The screw is inserted into the elliptical opening on the top of the floor plate catch and screwed onto the trigger guard. The spring is fitted into the "]" with one end being supported by the rear end of the floor plate catch housing. It constantly exerts forward pressure on the claw and prevents the claw from releasing the floor plate. When the floor plate catch is pulled to the rear, pressure is applied to the catch spring, and this disengages the catch from the floor plate, thereby causing the floor plate to drop open.

24. The trigger guard screw passes through the screw sleeve attached to the stock and connect to the rear end of the trigger guard to the rear end of the recoil plate. It is the longest screw in the trigger guard group.

E. Stock Group.

26. The rifle stock is made of walnut and its entire surface is lacquered.
The rifle stock is used to hold the rifle in firing and as a weapon with the bayonet. It is attached to the rifle by means of screw upper band and lower band. From the standpoint of convenience the stock is divided into three sections: Namely, the stock, grip and butt.

The stock has a cleaning rod chamber and cleaning rod catch housing in the front and a magazine housing on the rear. The screw hole located at the extreme front end of the stock is used for the upper band plate. The holes following are used for upper band and lower band, respectively

A small hole is provided at the rear right side for repair work and grooves are provided on both sides in order to facilitate holding when firing. The front end is notched to fit the upper band plate and upper band. Water drainage holes for the cleaning rod chamber are located at the front bottom section of the magazine housing.

The trigger slot is found at the rear. A longitudinal groove which accommodates the forward projection of the receiver is found in the upper forward section of the stock. An aperture for the buffer is located at the back end of this groove. Two vertical holes located in the groove which accommodates the front and rear projections of the receiver.

The lower band in the center of the stock is attached by means of the lower bank screws. Two narrow, long and service holes for the cleaning rod chamber are found in the rear, interior of the cleaning rod chamber. The grip section facilitates gripping the rifle during firing.

The butt is made from two materials held together by means of dovetail joints and is provided with butt sling swivel and butt plate. The forward end of the butt is reinforced by a recoil plate and trigger guard. The rear end of the bout is protected by the butt plate. A screw sleeve is inserted into the hole located at the rear of the recoil plate.

27. The stock attachments consist of upper ban plate, upper band, cleaning rod catch, hand guard catch (short rifle only) lower band, bugger, butt sling swivels, butt plate, hand guard and cleaning rod.

28. The upper bank plate covers the front end of the stock and is attached to the upper band by means of upper band plate screw. Its semicircular notch supports the barrel.

29. The upper band, together with the upper band plate, covers the head of the stock and compresses the barrel from the top. It is fitted to the cleaning rod catch base by means of two screws. The upper band plate is attached to the upper band by inserting upper band plate screws from right to left through the screw hold located in the forward section of the upper ban. The bayonet lug found on the lower portion of the upper band is used for attaching the bayonet.

30. The cleaning rod catch consists of the body, spring and seat. A hole for inserting the cleaning rod is made in the body and the seat. The spring fitted in the spring slot, constantly applies pressure to the cleaning rod catch and causes the hole of the seat and the hole of the body to lock. Thus, the body engages the recess of the cleaning rod and prevents the cleaning rod from slipping out. In order to release the cleaning rod the body is pressed inward to disengage the cleaning rod from the body and the cleaning rod is pulled out.

31. The hand guard catch is attached to the stock of the lower band section located on the forward end of the hand guard in such a way that it holds the barrel from the bottom. The upper surface of the hand guard catch clamps into the hand guard and together with the metal frame at the rear portion of the hand guard and prevents movement of the battle. It is attached to the stock by means of the lower band screw.

The lower band consists of the body, swivel, screw and monopod. The shape of the lower ban for rifles and short rifles is different.

The monopod consists of the body, mount, mount pin spring, spring pin and nut. The body is inserted into the mount and is engaged by the mount pin which connects the mount and the lower band. The spring is attached by spring pin and nut and from both sides, maintains the monopod in folded or erect position. When the monopod is folded etc. the front end hoods onto the upper band screw. The lowering the monopod is prevented by locking. The spring pin is inserted from the right side and locked from the left side with a nut.

The swivel for the rifle is attached to the bottom of the lower band and that of the short rifle to the left side of the lower band. It is used for attaching the sling. The monopod can be bent conventionally according to the nature of the terrain.

33. The buffer is an angular shaft, inserted, from right to left, into the buffer hold located in front of the magazine housing of the stock. It is locked on the left side by means of a nut. It sustains the forward projection of the receiver and together with the recoil plate transmits the recoil during fire to the stock.

34. The butt slings assembly consists of the seat and swivel. The seat is attached to the butt and the swivel to the seat. The butt swivel and lower band swivel are used to attach the sling. The shape and position of the butt sling assembly for the rifle and short rifle differ. In the case of the rifle, the butt sling assembly is attached to the bottom of the butt by means of long and short screw. Since the seat of the butt sling assembly for the short rifle is elevated to limit the forward tripping the swivel, the sling can be easily adjusted for slinging while wearing a gas mask.

35. The butt plate is attached to the end of the stock by means of long and short wood screws. It protects the butt and strengthens the joint of the two materials which form the butt.

36. The shape of the hand guard for the rifle and short rifle differ.

The hand guard for the rifle consists of the body and metal frame. It covers the barrel from the top, preventing its movement and protects the hand from grasping the firearm when the barrel is heated. Its forward edge is clamped by the lower band and the groove on its bottom surface fits of the hand guard catch. Its rear end, the inner surface of which is attached to a metal frame, is inserted into the front end of the rear sight base. The metal frame covers the barrel, and together with the hand guard catch, prevents the hand guard from moving.

The hand guard for the short rifle consists of the body and metal frame. It covers the barrel from the top and prevents it from moving and protects the hand in grasping the rifle when the barrel is heated. Its rear end, the inner surface of which is attached to a metal frame is inserted into the front end of the rear sight base. The metal frame coves the barrel from the top. Its front end is covered by the upper band, which together with the lower band prevent the hand guard from moving. The lower band is located about three and one half inches in front of the rear sight base and holds the hand guard and the stock together by means of a screw.

37. The cleaning rod is used for cleaning and stacking rifles. A male screw is provided at the bottom and a hole at the top end. When the occasion arises, cleaning rod jog, swab and auxiliary cleaning rod can be attached to the male screw. A piece of wood or cloth can be

inserted in the top hole to facilitate cleaning.

II Function of the Breech Mechanism

38. The relationship between the receiver and bolt during firing is:

(a.) When the bolt is opened and five rounds contained in the cartridge clip are loaded into the magazine located at the front of the receiver, the rounds depress the follower and stack three to the right and two to the left. The rounds are raise upwards by means of the magazine spring.

(b.) When the bolt is pushed forward the clip is released by the pressure exerted the bottom by the bolt. The uppermost round pushed from the rear, Slides up the cartridge ramp, located in front of the magazine port at the bottom of the receiver, and enters the chamber. At this moment the extractor engages the rim of the cartridge in preparation for extraction.

(c.) When the bolt is completely closed and the trigger pulled, the seat is lowers, disengaging it from the cocking lever. The compressed firing pin spring drives the firing pin forward until the firing pin strikes the primer of the cartridge.

At this time the bolt handle will not open since the safety lock has engaged the safety lock groove toe the bolt. Furthermore, when the breech is not closed properly, the trigger cannot be pulled since the safety lock will not be aligned with the groove. Thus, a safety measure is provided.

(d.) When the bolt handle is raised the bolt is drawn to the rear the ejector, by means of ejector springs, enters the groove of the bolt housing and ejects the cartridge, which has been extracted by the extractor. When the bolt is pulled fully back, it is prevented from slipping out of the receiver since the bolt catch engage the bolt retaining lug.

(e.) When the bolt is again brought forward, the next round is chambered, discharged and ejected in the same manner as the previous round.

(f.) When all of the rounds have been expended the follower catches the bolt face and prevents its advance. This indicated to the fired that the magazine is empty.

39. Safety can be maintained by the safety lock and safety knob. The function of the safety lock has previously been explained (c. of 30. The safety knob in operation prevents the bolt handle from opening and also locks the trigger. In short, the safety knob is operated in the following manner. When the safety knob is pressed forward, turned 45-degrees to the right the safety knob catch enters the curved groove in the rear of the receiver and locks the safety knob. When this is done, the small projection at the rear of the bolt handle engages the recess on the outer fringe of the safety knob and prevents the bolt handle and the bolt from

opening. At the same time, the firing pin turns with the safety knob, the sear catch moves from the firing pin catch, enters the left recess and disengages the firing pin from the sear, thereby locking the trigger

When the safety knob is locked, the position of the semicircular cut on the upper left of the safety knob is changed to an upward position.

Chapter 2 – Accessories

40. Accessories Include the Following:
1. Accessories bag
> Contents
> Lubricating cord
> Swab and swab container
> Cleaning rod tip
> Auxiliary cleaning rod.
> Cleaning rod guide.
> Cleaning rod.

2. Sling (long rifle and short rifle are different)

3. Ammunition pouch type A
> Front ammunition pouch
> Rear ammunition pouch

4. Ammunition pouch, Type B
5. Ammunition pouch Type C
6. Cartridge belt
7. Oil container Type B (1 ¼ ounces
9. Ammunition pouch Type A, B, and C.
> Cartridge belt
> Oil container, type A 2 ½ ounces
> Oil container Type B 1 ¼ ounces are used according to respective maintenance classification.

The accessories bag is made of canvas, measures ten-inches long and two and one-eighth inches wide. It is opened and closed by means of a buckle type strap and contains the following:

(1.) Lubricating cord
This is used to clean the bore when time allows during marches or combat. It consists of a hemp cord and weight with an overall length of one meter. When using, drop the weighted end into the bore, attach cleaning patch to loop on the opposite end and pull through to

clean or lubricate the bore.

(2.) Cleaning rod tip
This consists of the body and the cleaning rod tip spindle which is screwed onto the cleaning rod or the auxiliary cleaning rod. The bore is cleaned by wrapping a cleaning patch around the body which rotates.

(3.) Swab
This is made of brass, equipped with a brush (hog bristles) and a connecting tube with a female screw at the lower end. It is attached to the cleaning rod of the auxiliary cleaning rod and used in cleaning the bore. When not in use, it is kept in the metal swab container to protect the brush.

(4.) Cleaning rod
Made of brass, it is used to clean the bolt, receiver and other grooves. The slot serves in attaching cleaning patches.

(5.) Auxiliary cleaning rod
There are two rods. One with female screws and the other with male screws. The female screw joins into the cleaning rod and the male rod screws into the cleaning rod tip or swab when cleaning, the auxiliary rod is attached.

(6.) Cleaning rod guide
Made of cylindrical wood with a catch toward the end. When cleaning, this attaches to the receiver and the cleaning rod is thrust through it to prevented facing the bore. The catch fits onto the bolt handle slot located towards the rear of the receiver and prevent s movement of the cleaning rod guide.

42. The gun sling is attached to the swivel, located on the lower band and the butt by means of a snap fastener, buckle and loose strap. The length can be adjusted by means of the buckle. The sling for the short rifle differs in that is wider, 25mm shorter and equipped with a snap link at the lower end, which, together with the butt swivel, makes demounting the sling convenient.

43. Ammunition pouch, Type A, is the general nomenclature for two front ammunition pouches and on rear ammunition pouch. The front pouches consist of the body, belt loop, button, connecting strap, cover, and fastening loop and cover fastener. The rear ammunition pouch consists of the body, fastening loop, button (with seat), belt loop, cover, cover fastener, partition and fastener straps Type A and B. The belt loop is attached to the bayonet belt. The interior of each ammunition pouch is partition into two compartments which hold the ammunition wrapped in a paper container. The rear ammunition pouch is equipped with an exterior compartment for oil, container Type A (2 ½ ounces). There are two elliptical holes in the bottom to facilitate remove of the paper containers.

44. Ammunition pouch Type B consists of the body, belt loop, cover fastener button, fastening strip, buckle strap, button, cover, cover fastener strip, partition, fastening loop and the belt. The partition divides the interior into three compartments. The middle compartment holds oil container Type B (1 ¼) ounces and the side compartments hold the ammunition wrapped in a paper container. It is equipped with an exterior compartment which holds the cleaning rod and a cleaning rod tip. It is slung over the left should by means of the tightening strap (buckle, strap, button) and fastened around the waist by means of the belt.

45. Ammunition pouch Type C is ammunition Type B without the belt and tightening strap (buckle, strap, button).

46. The cartridge belt is made of canvas and reinforces on the top and bottom by leather. It is fastened around the waist by means of the buckle strap and tightening strap. It has large, medium and small pouches. There are two large pouches which hold one hand grenade each, six medium pouches which hold ten rounds of ammunition each and one small pouch which holds an oil container.

47. Oil container Type A consists of the body, applicator, cases A and B and screw cap. Oil container Type B consists of the body applicator, filling spout and cases A and B

Chapter 3.
Bayonet and Accessories

48. The bayonet and other steel parts are all blue. It consists of the blade (hilt, pommel, guard, hilt, grip, catch) and scabbard. The blade is straight with a blood groove on each side and an overall length of 20 inches. The hilt features a guard toward the blade and the pommel is riveted to it at the butt end. The bayonet lug groove is on the pommel which also houses the catch. The bayonet lug on the rifle fits into the bayonet lug groove and the action of the catch unites the rifle and the bayonet. The catch which is equipped with a spring is inserted into the catch housing from the right and fixed in place from the left by means of an escutcheon. The escutcheon is center punched. The end of the guard with the round hole is known as the dragon's head and when the bayonet is fixed the other end is known as the dragon's tail. The easily handled hilt grip is attached on both sides of the hilt by means of two sets of screws, seat, and escutcheon with the forward end adjoin the guard and the other end adjoining the pommel. The screws are inserted from the right and seated with the escutcheon form the left. The blade stem is 7 ½ inches in length from the forward end.

The scabbard consists of a mouth, scabbard catch, and a pointed tip. The mount reinforces the upper end of the scabbard. A plate spring is welded below this. The scabbard catch is attached below the mouth by means of a screw. The bayonet is fastened to the frog by means of the scabbard strip on the frog. The pointed tip is welded and protects the tip of the scabbard.

The plate spring which is located with the scabbard, sandwiches the blade and prevents it from slipping out.

49. Bayonet accessories include the frog and the belt. The bayonet is attached to the frog and the belt, which suspends the frog, is used to carry the bayonet as a sidearm. The frog is equipped with a buckle and a scabbard strip. The belt is equipped with a buckle and a scabbard strap. In the event the belt is too short for the user, there is a long belt Type A

Chapter 4.
Ammunition

50. The regular cartridge, Ball caliber .30 M2 consists of the cartridge case, primer, propellant powder and the bullet. The overall weight is 396 grains and its overall length is 3.34 inches. The case is mad e of brass. The bullet tip is plain and unmarked. The bullet is composed of a gilded metal with a lead core.

51. Cartridge Armor Piercing, cal. 30 M2. This cartridge is similar in appearance to the cartridge Call cal. 30 M2 except that the bullet tip is painted black. The bullet consists of a gilded metal jacket, a hard alloy steel core, a lead, T-shot point filler and a gilded metal, base filler.

52. Cartridge Trade cal.30 M1. This cartridge is used in rifle for signal and incendiary purposes, target designation, range estimation and target practice. This cartridge is readily identified by its red-tipped bullet indicating the color of its trace.

53. Cartridge tracer caliber .30 M25 (T-10). This cartridge is used in machineguns primarily but may be used in rifles also. The difference between this cartridge and the cartridge tracer caliber .30 M1 is that the bullet from this cartridge has dim trace up to approximately 100 yards. Then the bright trace begins and continues to approximately 1,000 yards. The color of this bullet tip is orange.

54. Cartridge blank caliber .30 M1909 this cartridge is used for simulated fire in maneuvers and exercises, signaling positions and firing salutes. It is readily identified since it has no bullet.

55. Cartridge dummy caliber .30 M2. This cartridge is used for training personnel in the operation of loading and unloading rifles and simulating rifle fire and in the inspection of weapons. It is easily identified by the three holes drilled in the cartridge and the absence of a primer.

56. Cartridge, rifle Grenade, caliber .30 M3. This cartridge is loaded with five grains of

black powder and for y grins of smokeless powder. This cartridge is only used with standard rifle grenade and grenade projection adapters. The length of the cartridge is 2.49 inches. The cartridge may be readily identified by the characteristic S-petal rose crimp of the mouth.

Part Two
Handling

Chapter 1
Disassembly and Assembly

57. There are two types of disassembly, regular and special. However, the special disassembly shall be limited to repairs and other necessary instances performed by Ordnance personal and the basic principal shall be that is not conducted din general. Also, the uses of arms and schools are prohibited disassemblies other than those mentioned in this chapter. Except in specially mentioned cases, the assembly shall generally be conducted in the reverse order to that of the disassembly.

As for the disassembly and assembly are concerned, the following must be noted carefully and any defective parts of the rifle must be repaired immediately.

I Normal disassembly and assembly

58. Parts that can be disassembled by the using unit.
Regular disassemblies are:
> Sling
> Belt
> Cleaning rod
> Follower spring and the follower

The assembly and disassembly of the sling are as follows:
(1.) In order to disassembly the rifle sling.
> (a.) Unfasten link catch and break the connection with the upper and.
> (b.) Lower the strip
> (c.) Unfasten the buckle.
> (d.) The sling becomes detached from the butt.

(2.) In order to assembly the rifle sling:
> (a) Slip the sling through the buckle.
> (b.) The sling is slipped through so that the stitches of the strap are on the left side of the rifle.
> (c.) Pass the end of the sling from the rear, through the butt sling swivel.
> (d.) Pass the strap through.
> (e.) Pass the end of the sling though the buckle from the front side.

(f.) Fasten at the appropriate eyelet.

(g.) Place the end of the sling into the strap.

(h.) Push the strap up until it is below the buckle.

(i.) Connect the front end of the sling with the lower band swivel.

(3.) Disassembly of the short rifle sling.

(a.) Unfasten the link button and detached form the lower band.

(b.) The removal of the buckle, strap and the spring catch are the same as with the rifle.

(c.) In the very end, the spring catch is detached from the butt sling swivel.

(4.) Assembly of the short rifle sling.

(a.) Fit the buckle.

(b.) Insert the strap.

(c.) Fit the spring catch so that the open and closed section faces the stock.

(d.) After this, the steps are the same as with the rifle.

60. In order to detach the bolt, place the rifle in the horizontal position with the barrel facing up. While supporting the rifle with the left hand, grasp the bolt handle with the right hand and placed in an upright position, pull it completely backward, then open the bolt catch to the left with the left thumb and pull the bolt handle slowly backward to remove from the receiver.

61. The bolt is disassembled in the following order aft the bolt cover is first removed.

62.

(1.) Safety knob

Hold the bolt with the left hand and place the palm of the right hand on the rear of the safety knob. Exert sufficient pressure on this and turn completely to the right. Then, if the pressure is released, the safety knob will become detached from the bolt housing.

(2.) Firing pin

Remove from the bolt housing

(3) Firing pin spring.

Remove from the striker.

(4.) Extractor

Grasp the bolt housing with the left hand. After moving the position of the extractor to above the elliptical hole, press he extractor forward and detach.

(5.) Precautions should be exercised in the following case in the disassembly and assembly of the bolt.

(a.) When removing the bolt, car should be taken so that the butt will not be damaged by the safety knob lug.

(b.) In assembly the extractor, align the extractor collar ears with the elliptical hole of the bolt housing. Fit the hold on the bottom surface of the extractor, and with the left hand grasp the bolt body together with the spring portion of extractor, then press the extractor outward with the right thumb and push into place which connects it with the extractor collar. After assembly, turn the extractor to the left and engage the projection behind the extractor hooks into the groove of the extractor housing, then place it accurately over the right locking lug of the bolt.

(c.) In inserting the firing pin into the bolt housing, the sear lug must be fitted into the rear semicircle otherwise it will be impossible to assembly the bolt.

(d.) In fitting the safety knob, the lug in the middle of the axle is fitted into the narrow groove on the inside of the rear part of the firing pin, then pressure is exerted. If it does not enter even after the application of pressure, turn slightly to the left or the right so that proper contact is made. After the safety knob enters, turn it completely to the left then relieve the pressure.

(e.) If the rear lug of the firing pin is fitted by mistake into the snail-shaped portion at the rear of the bolt housing, grasp the bolt housing with the left hand, press the safety knob sufficiently with the right hand and turn the sear lug to the right along the snail-shaped part. After it stops, reapply pressure and when the firing pin spring will move no further, the sear lug is fitted into the semicircular part. Then the safety knob is rotated to the left. It is no correctly assembled.

(f.) If through error the bolt is placed into the receiver without assembling the extractor, without forcing anything, first ascertain the position of the safety knob lug. Then after guiding it correctly to the right, extract the bolt slowly. When the extractor is being detached because of jamming during fire, after the extractor collar is moved to the right side, the bolt is pushed forward carefully and the extractor is engaged with the extractor collar. Then the bolt is pulled back. Also, when the empty cartridge case remains in the cartridge chamber due to jamming, a clean cleaning rod is inserted into the bore and the cartridge ejected before engaging the ejector.

(g.) When the bolt is fitted into the receiver, the correctness of the bolt assembly is recheck, the catches on both sides of the bolt covers are fitted into grooves on the outside of the receiver, the bolt retainer is opened outward, the bolt pushed forward, magazine platform depressed downward an assembly completed. Then the trigger is pulled the firing pin is left in the sear catch position.

62. In removing the follower spring and the follower, pull the floor plate catch. After the

floor plate opens, grasp it with the left hand. With the right hand, grasp the lower blade of the spring slightly above the bent portion, lift upward slightly and pull backward. Then it will become detached from the floor plate. The followers and the follower springs are also disassembled in the same manner.

II Special Disassembly and Assembly
(by Ordnance personnel only!)

64. Special disassembly is executed after the regular disassembly are:
> Front upper band and the upper band plate.
> Lower band.
> Hand guard.
> Barrel and receiver (base maintenance only)
> Magazine
> Floor plate catch
> Cleaning rod catch
> Butt plate
> Butt sling swivel.
> Monopod

65. The order of the special disassembly is as follows:

(a.) Front sight base and front sight.
After the caulked pin is extracted from right to left, the seat is tipped forward. The sigh can b pounded out either from the left or right. Care must be exercise not to damage the front sight lade. When reassembled the rifle must be zeroed in again, the old marker line erased and replaced by new marker line.

(b.) Upper band and the upper band plate.
Remove the left and right screws and the plate bolt and detach with the plate.

(c.) Lower Band
Place the barrel facing left, unscrews the small screw and remove together with the monopod.

(d.) Hand guard
Barrel is placed facing upward. Gasp the front end of the hand guard and remove together with its metal frame by pulling slowly to the front while slightly lifting upwards.

(e.) Barrel and receiver
After removing the long and short receiver screws and the trigger guard screw, place the rifle in a level position with the barrel facing up. Grasp the receiver with the

right hand and the front sight section with the left hand then remove upward. Next detach the recoil plate.

In order to disassemble the rear sight, the rear axle pin is removed and the rear sight detached. The rear sight spring is disassembly from the base by removing the small rear sight sprig screw and tipping it slightly forward.

In the disassembly of the slide, first remove the small rear sight screw and detach the slide from the rear sight. Next, unscrew the left and right slide catch pins, then detach the slide catches and slide catch arms from the slide. In the disassembly of the antiaircraft lead sight arms, the antiaircraft lead sight arm screws are unscrewed and the arms removed. The springs are next detached. The spring will become detached if pulled about three millimeters from the outside inward.

In the disassembly of the rear sight base, the rear sight base screw is removed and the base pulled out to the fore. In the disassembly of the bolt retainer and the ejector, after pulling out the bolt retainer spring, unscrew the bolt retainer pin. Then detach the bolt retainer from the receiver and the ejector from the bolt retainer. The ejector spring is inserted in the bolt retainer latch spring. In disassembling the sear and the trigger, the sear pin is extracted then the sea and the trigger are detached from the receiver. Next the trigger pin is removed and the trigger detached from the sear.

(f.) Magazine
In the disassembly of the magazine, the trigger guard is detached from the stock, the front pin extracted and the floor plate removed from the trigger guard. Then the magazine can be readily disassembly as it is merely inserted into the magazine chamber in the stock.

When assembling the magazine, place the lower side toward the front and the angular side facing up.

(g.) Floor plate catch
The floor plate catch is disassembly by removing a small screw to the rear of the trigger guard, then pulling it out together with the spring.

(h.) Cleaning rod catch
The cleaning rod catch is removed by pushing it inward from the outside. In such cases the base and the spring of the cleaning rod catch disassemble together form the stock.

(i.) Butt plate
The butt plate is disassembly by unscrewing the wood screws. When assembling, the longer wood screw is screwed in at the lower end and the shorter wood screw is screwed in

at the top.

(j.) Butt sling swivels

The butt sling swivel is disassembled by removing the wood screws. With the rifle, the longer wood screw is screwed in on the side that is closer to the front end and the shorter wood screw on the side that is closer to the rear end. With the short rifle, the slanted surfaced is placed facing the rear end. Be sure that error is not made as to the front and rear sides.

(k.) Monopod

The monopod is disassembly from the lower band, the spring pin and nut are removed then the spring detached. The monopod base pin is removed then the monopod is detached from the lower band as the monopod from the monopod base.

66. Care must be exercised in the special disassembly and assembly of the following cases.

(a.) During the disassembly and assembly of the upper and lower bands the bluing of the barrel must not be scraped off and the stock must not be damaged.

(b.) During the disassembly of the hand guard, care must be taken in order not to damage the metal frame and the rear end.

(c.) When removing the barrel and receiver, the front and the rear must be removed evenly from the stock, otherwise the sock may be damaged.

(d.) The barrel and receiver are disassembled only when replacement of the barrel is necessary.

(e.) When the trigger guard screws and the receiver screws are being screwed in, be sure they are turned evenly, otherwise the trigger guard may become tilted and cannot be properly tightened. Also when the small screw is not tightened properly it negatively affects the accuracy of the rife. When firing, the contact point between the stock and the receiver is often damaged when the barrel recoils.

(f.) During assembly, the pins and screws must be inserted in the directions stipulated.

Chapter 2
Precautions in Handling

67. The point to be noted in the tests about to be mentioned below is that the easily damaged parts must be handled with care. Although the other details are identical to those described in the manual on the preservation of arms, the main points are:

68. The muzzle, front sight, rear sighs and the bolt must not be allowed to touch the ground.

69. When the rifle is not in use the bolt is closed and the firing pin is placed in the after fire position.

The use of wood paper, cloth etc. as a cap for the muzzle must be avoided because of the possibility of damage to the barrel.

70. The ammunition is first loaded into the magazine and then inserted into the chamber by the bolt. When the ammunition is placed directly into the chamber and the bolt closed the extractor will be damaged.

71. After exposure to dust, the bore (conditions permitting) should be cleaned before firing. The muzzle section should be spot checked.

72. When exposed to rain or snow the bore must be cleaned as soon as time permits. The presence of moisture in the interior of a rifle promotes rusting.

73. The plugging of the muzzle with Vaseline or grease in order to prevent the entry of water into the bore must be avoided because if fired while plugged, it may cause the barrel to burst or bulge.

74. If the monopod is bent during use, it is correct by the soldier himself if possible.

75. Precautions that should be taken in subzero areas:

(a.) If misfire occur frequently, wipe the oil from the bolt assembly.

(b.) When keeping the rifle indoors after use, proper oil must be applied to it. The slings must be kept away from fires and it is also necessary to take precautions against freezing as the leather sling cracks easily

(c.) During the period a rifle is not in use, it must be kept in a warm place or indoors ad much as possible to prevent it from freezing. If kept outdoors unavoidably, it must be covered with a blanket or a straw mat. If possible a fire should be built to prevent any trouble when called upon for unexpected firing.

(1.) When a rifle is carried in from out of doors, the change of temperature induces moisture to form on the metallic parts causing it to rust. Therefore, it must wiped off: The bore especially must be cleaned.

(2) The humidity of building in subzero areas equipped with heaters becomes exceedingly

low and unless the stock is oiled, it will become excessively dry. As this causes the stock to warp, the rifle rack must be placed in a position as far as possible from the heater and humidity must be maintained at the proper level.

76. The following precautions must be exercised in tropical areas.

(a.) If conditions permit, open the bolt frequently while firing and cool by ventilating with the bore in order to aid in the dissipation of heat.

(b.) Exposure to direct sunlight heats the gun causing the wooden parts to warp. Therefore, if conditions permit, place in the shade or in a location with a steady draft.

Chapter 3
Packing

77. In packing rifles, in addition to the consideration of the method of shipping and the distance, it is necessary to take into consideration the weather and the season before deciding on the degree and the method.

78. The following precautions should be taken with the inner packing.

(a.) Dip the rifle in preservative (Cosmoline) as directed in TM 9-850

(b.) It is necessary that the supports and braces of the crate be rigidly fixed to prevent any damage to the contents when the crate is placed on its side, overturned or jarred while in transit.

Chapter 1
Care

77. The care is generally as follows;
Care of the bore and chamber
Care of the bolt mechanism
Care of the other parts of the rifle and the wooden parts.
Care of the leather articles
Care of linen and cotton goods.

80. In the care of the bore place the rifle in a level position on a stand or a rack. Remove the bolt. Insert the cleaning rod fitted with the cleaning rod guide or a cleaning rod fitted with a clean rod tip on which a patch is tied, into the bore and move it slowly forwards and backwards. After repeating this several times (and when the bore is clean) apply a thin coat of oil in the same manner.

When cleaning a rifle rotated the cleaning rod tip to follow the rifling. Moreover it is necessary to revolve the rifle appropriately in order to prevent the rubbing of any one particular spot in the bore.

Be careful so that the cleaning rod tip and the cleaning rod do not directly rub against the surface of the bore. At the same time, check to see if this is conducted correctly and avoid the use of bent rods.

The care of the chamber consists of inserting the chamber cleaning rod fitted with a rag in the slot on it front and in order to remove the old oil or to apply fresh oil

As the bore I chromium plated, excessive cleaning is unnecessary. Therefore, it is necessary to observe the condition of the bore and the stain on the rag and adopt a suitable method and frequency of cleaning.

81. In the care of the bolt assembly, after the old oil and dust have been removed from each part, apply oil somewhat more heavily on the worn parts of the bolt by means of a brush, an oily rag and lightly on other parts.

The use of a cleaning rod in the cleaning and oiling of the inside and outside of the bolt housing, corners, grooves and the housing of the firing pin spring is recommended.

Since the bolt face is chromium-plated, as is the bore of the barrel, care must be exercise in handling it.

82. Old oil and dust are removed from the other steel parts with a rag after which oil is applied with an oily rag. A somewhat greater amount of oil is applied to the pins and functioning parts. The exposed surfaces of the wood parts are cleaned with a rag. Any oil that adheres to the wood parts will be wiped off.

83. It is necessary to adjust the amount of oil applied because if an excessive amount is applied, it not only increases the adherence of dust, but the excess accumulates in the lower parts and leaks out onto he stoke cause it to become stained Moreover it may be blown into the eyes of the gunner when firing.

84. Leather goods are cared for by applying a thin film of Neat's-Foot Oil on the top surfaces with a piece of rag. Apply sparingly then wipe off the excess with a dry cloth.

When applying oil to the leather slings, it must be rubbed crosswise and not lengthwise.

Any oil remaining on textile fabric products must be removed as it damages the fibers.
If any mildew is detected, clean immediately with either a dry or moist cloth. However,

this method is not adequate, care must be exercised because it frequently promotes further growth. Moreover, a rag once use to remove mildew must not be used on other unaffected leather parts.

85. Soiled web canvas products are washed in soapy water.

86. Even during fire, the rifle is cleaned and cared for as conditions permit.

II Care Before Firing

87. Care before fire consists of a thorough cleaning of the bore and chamber followed by an application of a thin film of oil. An application of an excessive amount of oil becomes a hindrance. When firing blank ammunition a somewhat greater amount of oil should be applied.

III Care After Firing

88. As the quality of after fire care greatly influences the preservation of the rifle, it is necessary to exercise special care. In addition to the general daily care, the following care must be rendered:

(a.) When exposed to gas, wash the contaminated parts as soon as possible with the bore cleaning fluid or a soapy solution, using a swab, or clean with bore oil.

(b.) After removing the contaminant and dirt with a rag, apply oil.

(c.) When the parts directly exposed to gas such as the bolt face, firing pin housing and the striker are left without cleaning, it hinders firing. Moreover, it results in corrosion, making proper care especially necessary.

(d.) If time is not available for proper care immediately following fire, apply a liberal quantity of oil with a thong, temporarily preventing corrosion and at the same time loosening the contaminant making cleaning later easier.

(e.) Every effort must be made to remove the fouling adhering to the bore surface. Rifle bore cleaner and wire brush are used for this purpose.

IV Care During Special Instances

89. Precautions to be taken in extremely hot areas are generally as follow:

As the flow and vaporization of oil and the rusting of the steel parts are hastened under extremely hot conditions, care must be exercised in the selection of the oil. The amount of oil applied and the frequency of application must be increased and the rifle kept in a horizontal position when not in use to prevent the oil from running off.

90. Precautions to be taken in extremely cold areas are generally as follows:

(a.) The freezing of oil applied to mechanical parts hinders functioning at extremely low temperatures, wipe the bolt dry. A rifle cleaned of its oil must not be left indoors without oiling due to the danger of rusting.

(b.) Conduct a dry run preceding fire to test the striking force of the firing pin. If this is weak, inspect for anything unusual about their parts, the actual resistance of the firing pin spring, then correct these to prevent the occurrence of trouble in firing.

(c.) Trouble may arise if a mixture of powder fouling and oil is frozen or stuck to the parts in the bolt housing. The removal of these becomes difficult after the rifle cools. Therefore, if possible, the rifle should be cleaned during the firing period or immediately following fire.

91. Precautions to be taken when the dust is severe:

(a.) in order to prevent adhesion and penetration of dust, application of oil to external parts must be minimized.

(b.) When the possibility of sand penetration is great, the bore must be cleaned frequently with an oiled cloth, tied loosely to the cleaning rod. The cloth must be changed often. The bore must be oiled only after it is absolutely free of sand. If the daily cleaning procedure is used from the start, the possibility of damage and wear to the bore is great since it would be like rubbing the bore with polishing powder. When the bore is being cleaned from the muzzle end, special care in the cleaning must be directed to the cartridge chamber since the sand from the bore will accumulate in the cartridge chamber.

99. Precautions to be taken during rain and show:

In rain and snow oiling must be done only after the moisture has been completed wiped off with a dry cloth. This operation must be conducted repeatedly.

Chapter 2:
Storage

93. The purpose of storing arms is to take appropriate measures to preserve them for long or short periods in order that they may be used again without any breakdown. The method

of storage and the handling of stored goods is prescribed in Technical Manual 9-850 United States Army and will be followed.

Chapter 3:
Inspections

I General Inspection.

A. Care
94. Principal points of inspection:

(a.) Barrel
(1.) Foreign matter (rust, pits and corrosion.
(2.) Metal fouling adhesion.

(b.) Receiver
(1.) Check to see if bolt locking lug housing, gas port and ejector housing are properly cleaned and oiled.

(c.) Bolt
        (1.)   Adhesion of foreign matter on bolt fact, firing pin, chamber and gas port.
        (2) Corrosion and rust in the firing pin hole.

(d.) Firing pin
Corrosion and rust on striker, adhesion of foreign matter on firing pin spring.

(e.) Leather and hemp items:
        (1.) Softness
        (2) Elasticity
        (3.) Hardness
        (4.) Mildew
        (5.) Dirt

If the leather strap should crack when it is rolled up between the fingers, it indicates insufficient oiling. If oil should seep from the leather when it is unrolled, excessive oiling is indicated.

B.
Assembly

95. Principal points of Inspections.
        (1.) Loose barrel
        (2.) Loose upper/lower band

(3.) Loose screws on upper/lower band
(4.) Faulty bending and faulty spring of monopod.
(5.) Loose upper plate
(6.) Malfunction of cleaning road.
(7.) Unusual projection, deflection and looseness of the trigger guard.
(8.) Loose magazine.
(9.) Loose trigger guard screw and long/short screws for receiver.
(10.) Loose wood screws for butt plate and butt sling swivels.
(11.) Use of wrong part numbers.

C Function
(1.)   Malfunction of safety knob.

96. Principal points of Inspection:
(1.) Malfunction of safety knob.
(2.) Malfunction of safety lock.
(3.) Malfunction of safety extractor.
(4.) Malfunction of safety ejector.
(5.) Malfunction of safety follower.
(6.) Thru (14) Faulty trigger mechanism
(15.) Faulty function of bayonet in mounting and dismounting

   C. Damage

97 Principal points of inspection:
(a.) Bore and chamber
(1.) Bulge
(2.) Pits
(3.) Bend
(4.) Wear
(5.) Dents

(b.) Receiver
(1.) Weak bolt lugs and ejector springs
(2.) Dent on bolt face.
(3.) Dent around snail-shaped section.
(4.) Wear on lower surfaces of bolt

(c.) Bolt
(1.) Enlargement of firing pin hole
(2.) Dent on bolt face
(3.) Dent around snail-shaped section
(4.) Wear on lower surface of bolt

(d.) Firing pin
    (1.) Bend wear on firing pone: malformation of striker point.
    (2.) Wear and tear on sear catch.
    (3.) Excessive projection on bolt face (projection should range between .044 and .049 thousands of an inch.
    (4.) Bent weak or sagging firing pin spring.

(e.) extractor and safety knob
      (1.) Wear on extractor claw and weak extractor spring.
      (2.) Loose safety knob shaft and wear in safety knob lug.

(f.) Front Sight
      (1.) Loose front sight base.
      (2.) Deflection of front sight.
      (3.) Bent or worn front sight.

(g.) Rear sight
      (1.) Faulty rear sigh pin.
      (2.) Malfunction of rear sight.
      (3.) Loose peep sight.
      (4.) Loose and creaky slide with irregular graduations.
      (5.) Dented peep sight.
      (6.) Peeled rust proof coating (peep sight and front sight).
      (7.) Loose antiaircraft lead sight arms.
      (8.) Bent antiaircraft lead sight arms.
        (9.) Weak and bent antiaircraft lead sight arm spring.

(h.) Stock

      (1.) Cracked and dented stock.
      (2.) Enlarged groove for recoil plate (1/32 of an inch allowed).
      (3.) Bent stock.
      (4.) Cracked and loose hand guard.
      (5.) Bent cleaning rod, loose cleaning rod head, worn thread.
      (6.) Broken snap ring for sling.

(i.) Leather and Hemp Items
      (1.) Cracks.
      (2.) Scars and damage.
      (3.) Unraveled seams.

(j.) Accessories
    (1.) Cracked and bent cleaning rod jog, worn threads and corroded steel section.
    (2.) Bent and worn cleaning rod.
    (3.) Damages to screw cap for oil can, weak oil can case and oil can leaks.

II Inspection Before and After Firing

98.   Before and after firing, various parts, especially the bore and chamber, special inspection must be made for the presence of foreign matter in the bore and chamber before firing.

Prior to zeroing-in, damaged parts which will affect the accuracy of the zeroing pin must be made on the changer bolt face, bolt locking lugs, firing pin head, extractor and bolt retaining lug housing.

III. Inspection of Stored Rifles

99. Prior to storage, special attention must be paid to the presence of dust, matching part numbers, proper function and a proper application of preservative. Bore and chamber must be examined with special thoroughness.

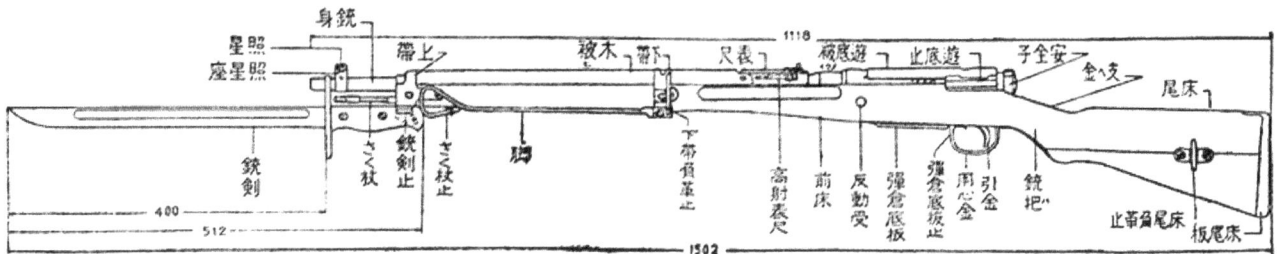

TOP

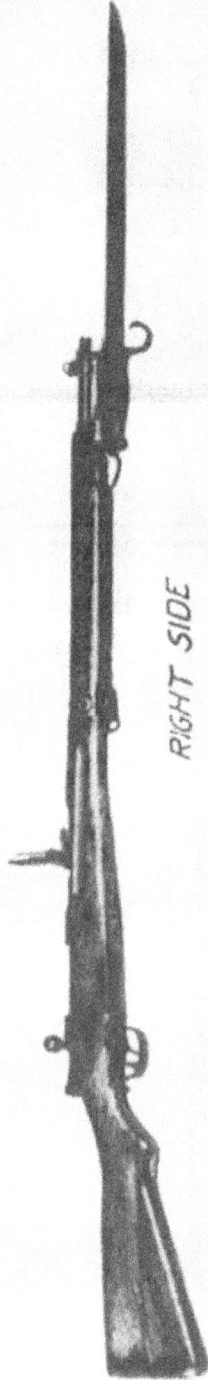

RIGHT SIDE

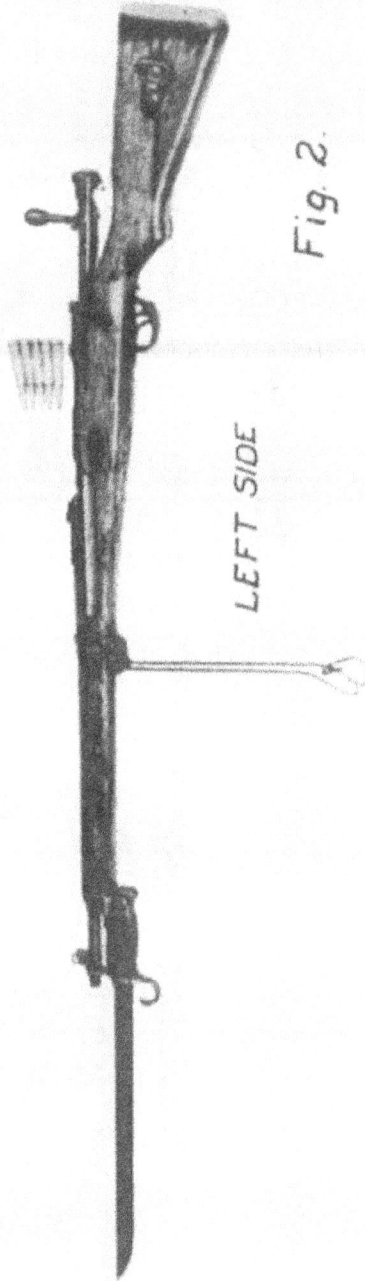

LEFT SIDE

Fig. 2.

38

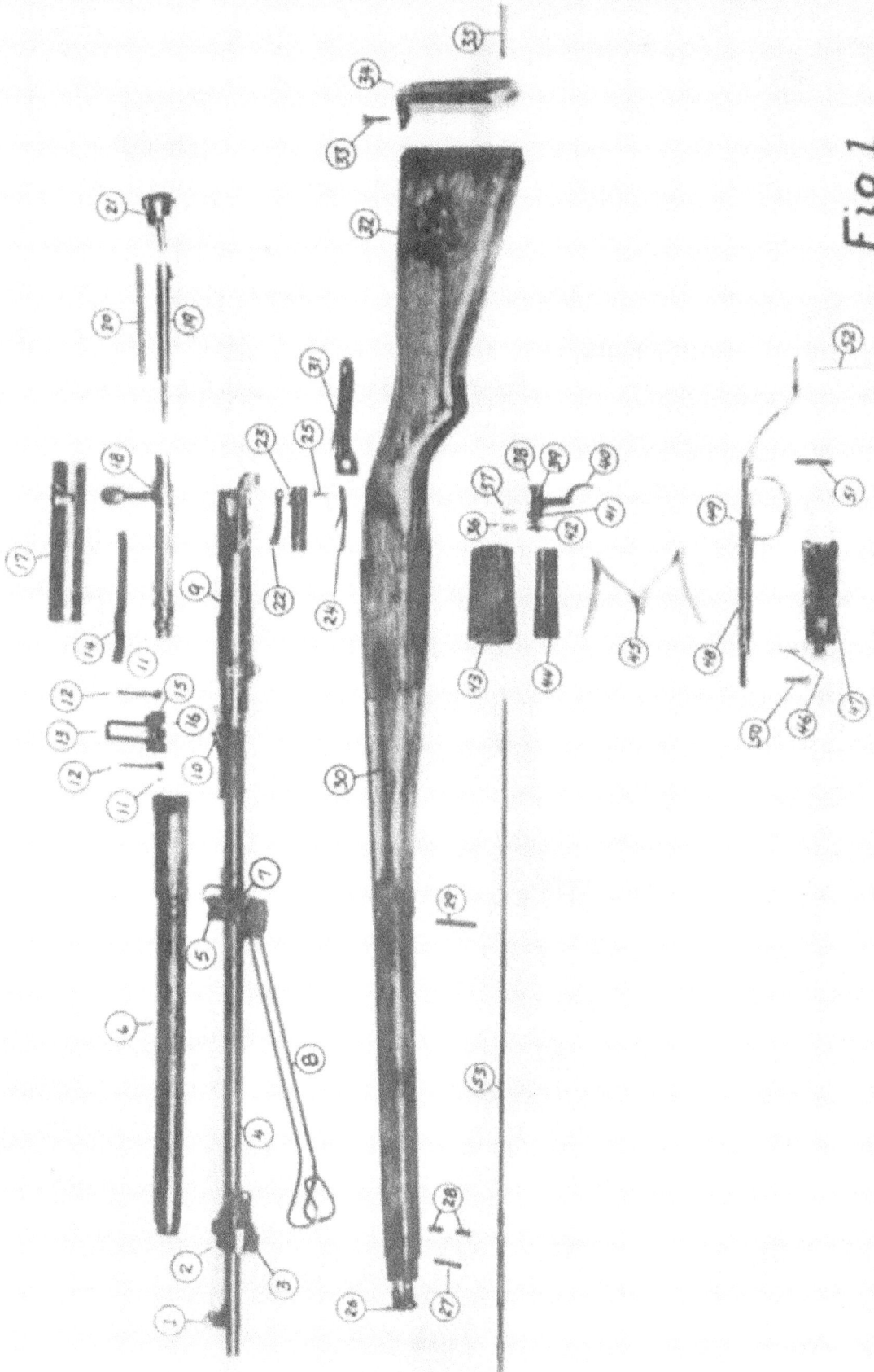

Fig.1.

NOMENCLATURE LIST

1. Sight, front
2. Band, upper
3. Lug, bayonet
4. Barrel
5. Band, lower
6. Guard, hand
7. Swivel, sling
8. Monopod
9. Receiver
10. Spring, rear sight
11. Screws, antiaircraft leading sight arm
12. Arms, leading sight anti-aircraft
13. Leaf, rear sight
14. Extractor
15. Slide, rear sight
16. Pin, cover rear sight
17. Cover, bolt
18. Bolt housing
19. Pin, firing
20. Spring, firing pin
21. Knob, safety
22. Ejector
23. Latch, bolt retainer
24. Spring, latch, bolt retainer and spring ejector
25. Screw, latch, bolt retainer
26. Plate, upper band
27. Screw, upper band plate
28. Screws, upper band
29. Screw, lower band
30. Stock-butt
31. Plate, recoil
32. Swivel, lower sling
33. Screw short, butt plate
34. Plate, butt
35. Screw, long butt plate
36. Spring, sear
37. Pin rocker arm
38. Sear
39. Pin, trigger
40. Trigger
41. Rocker arm
42. Guide, sear spring
43. Magazine
44. Follower
45. Spring, follower
46. Pin, floor plate
47. Plate, floor
48. Guard, trigger
49. Catch, floor plate
50. Screw, forward trigger guard
51. Screw, rear trigger guard
52. Screw, recoil plate
53. Rod, cleaning

MIDDLE COAST
PUBLISHING

Middle-Coast-Publishing.com

On the following pages is a catalog of our Military Firearms Series of Books, all of which are available at Amazon Books.

FREDERIC FAUST

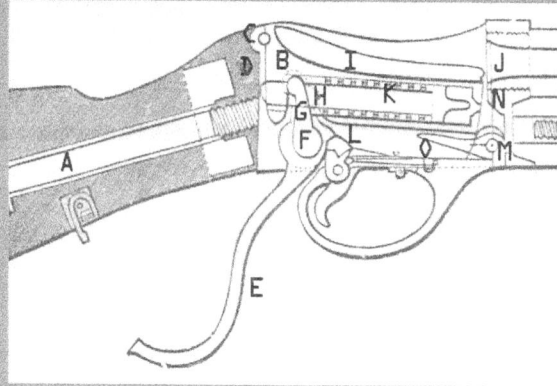

The Lineage of the Martini-Henry Rifle

Facts and Circumstances in the History and Development of the Martini-Henry Rifle

ISBN-13: 978-0934523-56-1

The Martini–Henry breech-loading single-shot lever-actuated rifle, entered British Army service in 1871. Martini–Henry variants, used throughout the British Empire for 30 years, combined the dropping-block action first developed by Henry O. Peabody (in his Peabody rifle) and improved by the Swiss designer Friedrich von Martini, combined with the polygonal barrel rifling designed by Scotsman Alexander Henry. Find out the details on exactly how these rifles work and who was Martini and who was Henry.

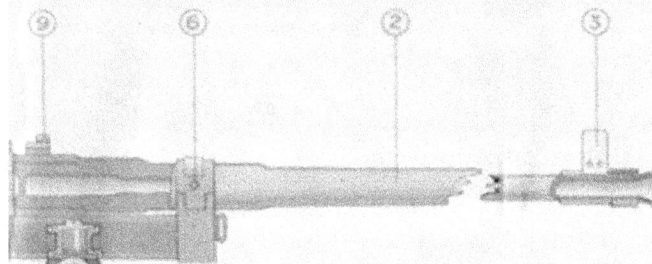

K RIFLE MK

ARMOURER'S NOTES:
BOYS ANTI-TANK RIFLE
With
Parts Listing and Diagrams

8 PISTOL GRIP.
9 BACKSIGHT BRACKET AND BACKSIGHT.
10 CHEEK REST.
11 SHOULDER PIECE.
12 SHOULDER PIECE GRIP.
13 OIL BOTTLE.

ISBN: 97809344523-6-46

Armourer's Notes: Boys Anti-tank Rifle explains to troops how to employ and maintain the Boys Anti-Tank Rifle. Coverage includes a breakdown of the weapon by salient groups, showing a diagram of each individual parts and identifying those parts by name and stock number.

LEE-ENFIELD

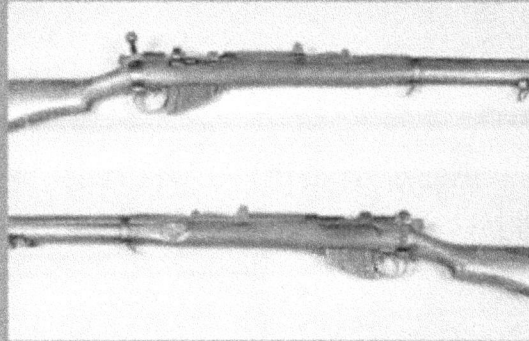

INSTRUCTIONS FOR ARMOURERS

Rifles No. 1, No. 2, and Rifle No. 3 (Pattern 14)

ISBN-13: 978-0934523-11-0

British War Office notes, circa 1931, on the SMLE provide unit armourers with detailed information on how to: Strip and reassemble the bolt and magazine; Clean a rusty barrel, Clear an obstructed bore, Check headspace, Replace a bolt head, Adjust trigger pull, Troubleshoot misfires, Fit a new striker, Blacking sights, and Fit a new fore end.

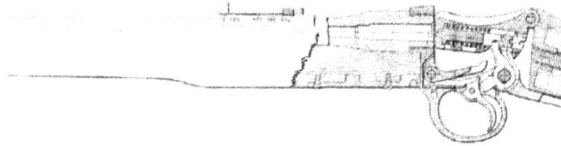

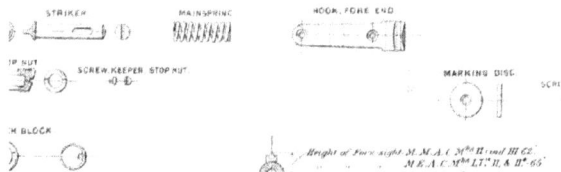

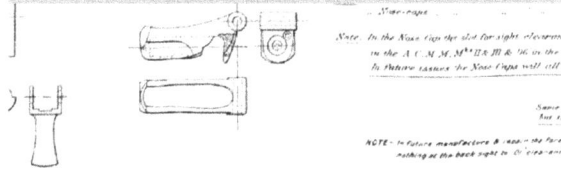

INSTRUCTIONS
FOR ARMOURERS
MARTINI-HENRY
Frederic Faust

ISBN-13: 978-0934523-55-4

Get genuine Martini-Henry gunsmithing techniques from the primary source, the British Army, circa 1897. This armourer's text tells exactly how to maintain and care for your rifle, from assembly and disassembly to simple fixes to the breech block and trigger.

LEE-ENFIELD RIFLE
EXPLODED DRAWINGS
AND PARTS LISTS

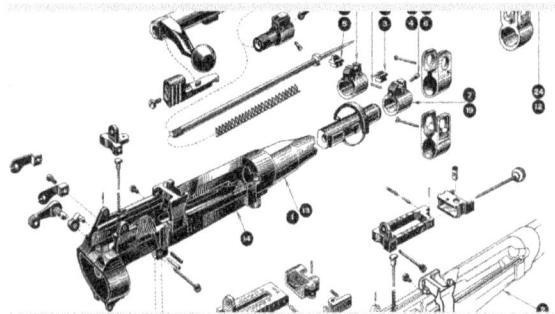

RIFLES NO. 1 MARK III (SMLE) - NO. 3
(PATTERN 14) - NO. 4 MARKS I & MARKI*

FREDERIC FAUST

ISBN-13: 978-0934523-63-9

This copiously illustrated Reprint of a 1945 War Department document shows each rifle by way of exploded drawings of the main components and sub-assemblies. Each part is identified by name and number. Published in large format (8 X 10).

LEE-ENFIELD RIFLE NO. 4 MARK I*

PHANTOM PARTS DIAGRAMS AND PARTS LISTING

FREDERIC FAUST

ISBN-13: 978-0934523-65-3

Built at the Canadian Long Branch Arsenal many aficionados consider the old warhorse to be the best of all the variants fielded during the Second World War. This book contains parts identification lists detailing by illustration, descriptive part name and part number, for all parts of the Rifle, .303 Calibre, Lee -Enfield, No 4, Mark 1 * and its associated equipment including bayonet, frog, action cover, wire gauze and pull-through. Parts are listed to show major assemblies, sub-assemblies, and component parts.

DEPARTMENT OF THE ARMY

FM 23-5

U. S. Rifle Caliber .30 M1

ISBN: 978-0934523-09-7

Profusely illustrated, this Department of the Army **REPRINT** is a guide in the instruction and training in the mechanical operation of the M1 Garand rifle, once described by General George S Patton as The Greatest Battle Implement ever devised. Coverage includes detailed description of the rifle, general characteristics; procedures for disassembly and assembly; methods of loading; an explanation of functioning; a discussion of stoppages and immediate action; a description of the ammunition; and instructions on the care and cleaning of both the weapon and ammunition.

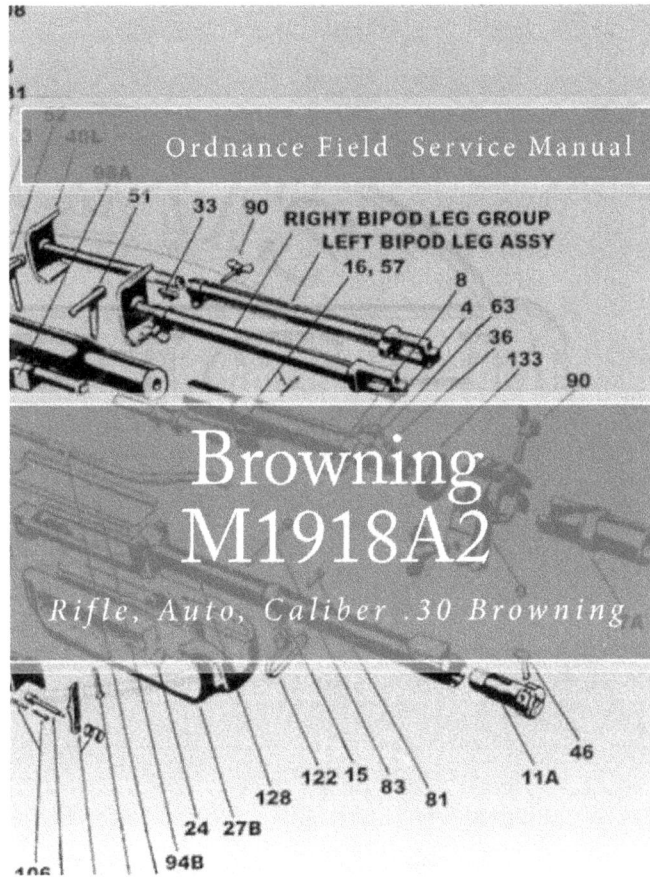

ISBN-13: 978-1541187-51-1

This comprehensive, large format reprint of a Rock Island Arsenal manual shows by way of phantom drawings all of the venerable BAR's parts and how they fit together.

U.S ARMY TECHNICAL MANUAL
Type 99 Arisaka
Caliber .30

Korean War Reprint
Colonel Arisaka
Nakiakiara

ISBN: 978-0934523-68-4

During the Korean War, approximately 126,500 short and 6,650 long Type 99 Rifles were re-chambered under American supervision at the Tokyo arsenal to fire the U.S. Military M2 -.30-06 Springfield cartridge. These rifles were fitted with a lengthened magazine well and had a small notch cut in the top of the receiver ring in order to accommodate the .30-06 round's 1/3 of an inch greater overall length. The Pentagon rather wisely wrote a Technical Manual for the converted rifles that addresses inspection of the weapon, care, assembly and function. This then is that TM.

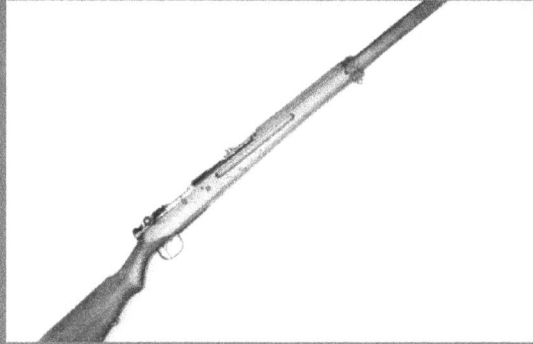

FREDERIC FAUST

The Lineage of the Arisaka

Facts and Circumstance in the History of the Arisaka Family of Rifles

ISBN: 978-0934523-32-5

The Arisaka family of Japanese military bolt-action service rifles, in production and use from 1897 until the end of World War II in 1945. The most common specimens include the Type 38 chambered for the 6.5×50mmSR Type 38 cartridge and the Type 99 chambered for the 7.7×58mm Type 99 cartridge. Many thousands of Type 99s and other Arisaka variants were brought to the United States by soldiers as war trophies during and after World War II. Find out about the rifle's namesake Colonel Arisaka and learn the fascinating history of this esteemed battle rifle.

EDITED BY FREDERIC FAUST

The Lineage of the Lee-Enfield Rifle

Facts and Circumstance in the
History of the .303 British

ISBN-13: 978-0934523-30-1

This book chronicles the history and development of the family of the venerable Lee-Enfield rifle, beginning in 1895 with a redesign of the Lee-Metford. On its pages you'll learn what an SMLE is and what is not, find out which countries carried it and which wars it fought in plus consult the registry of serial numbers for Rifles No. 4 and No. 5.

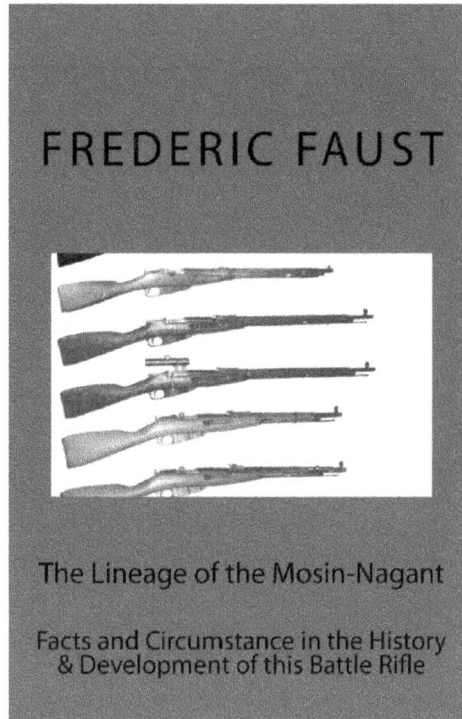

FREDERIC FAUST

The Lineage of the Mosin-Nagant

Facts and Circumstance in the History & Development of this Battle Rifle

ISBN-13: 978-0934523-15-8

The Mosin–Nagant is a five-shot, bolt-action, internal magazine-fed, military rifle, developed by the Imperial Russian Army in 1882–91 and used by the armed forces of the Russian Empire, the Soviet Union and various other nations.

It is one of the most mass-produced military bolt-action rifles in history with over 37 million units produced since its invention in 1891. And in spite of its age, it has pulled duty in various armed conflicts around the world even up to the modern day. This comes as no big surprise when considering how these rifles are plentiful, cheap, rugged, simple to use, and effective, much like the AK-47 and its variants.

Find out about the parts played by the rifles namesakes Mosin and Nagant. Learn all about the fascinating history and evolution of this esteemed battle rifle.

www.ingramcontent.com/pod-product-compliance
Lightning Source LLC
Chambersburg PA
CBHW080533030426

42337CB00023B/4711